Parent
Alex Gallagher

nthetica
?dBodie
enthetj
poBBod

First published 2017
Reprinted 2019
by Subbed In

© Alex Gallagher 2019

Cover design by Dan Hogan
Book design by Sam Wieck
Text set in 8pt Domaine Text

Second edition

Printed and bound in Birraranga (Melbourne)

National Library of Australia Cataloguing-in-Publication:
Gallagher, Alex
Parenthetical bodies / Alex Gallagher.
ISBN: 9780648147510 (paperback)

Subbed In 002

www.subbed.in

CONTENTS

"Do what you want, don't hurt anyone;
if you love someone, take care of them"
— Hannahband

vague

imagining myself as a sketch of a person
messy strokes around a vague outline
the details fill out when you kiss the space
between my neck and collarbone

they fade when the woman at the grocery store asks if
"that will be all today, sir"

i'm tired of feeling broken by language
when it is the only safe place i've ever known

wrapping myself up in its coat to feel secure
digging its fingernails into my skin to feel held

surviving on the promise that
some elusive cryptographic combination
could make things right

that i could articulate the things
words don't exist for yet;
how having a body is exhausting

people assume my problem
is that i'm a woman trapped in a man's body
when the problem is more like
i'm trapped in a body

to become is to break yourself apart,
i remind myself each time i leave the house

it's supposed to hurt this much

gossamer

it is hard to let yourself stay tender
in a place with edges so sharp

wearing a gossamer gown
through a forest of flick knives

the terrified pedestrian
crossing petrified pavement,

nestled into the enclaves
that envelope the body

agitated car alarms echo
fill each fraction and gap

dare anyone hold some silence
between the lines of their palms

cut out the ugly things inside of you
in order to survive an uglier place

the earth screams constantly
because it is trying to scare you into submission;

but you dig your heels in,
you are a survival expert

hold tight to empathy
knowing it is not weakness

to have endured all you have,
to still have a fully beating heart to show for it

surf's up

right now
i am a dog wearing sunglasses

more specifically,
i am a dog wearing sunglasses
on a surfboard

i am a dog wearing sunglasses
on a surfboard, wearing a leather jacket

i am a dog wearing sunglasses
wearing a leather surfboard,
riding a wave of disappointment

i am a dog wearing disappointment

i am the wave,
i am a disappointed dog,
and there's nothing sadder on this earth
than a disappointed dog

last night your new girlfriend saw me at the grocery store
buying a large bag of doritos for myself
and a salsa jar that said "great for parties"
which, also, was for myself

it was weird

it could have been a party if we'd eaten it together
but instead we just pretended not to see each other

now it's later,
i am a surfboard wearing a leather jacket

i am a surfboard riding a wave of leather jackets
to be eaten by sharks who have no idea
how cool they might look
wearing a leather disappointment

i am a dog wearing a leather shark
this morning we went to the beach
and i asked what you were hopeful for
and you said you were hopeful because you met me

unfortunately,
i am a disappointment wearing sunglasses

i am a dog wearing sunglasses

you can't send
me to feelings jail
(i'm already in
feelings hell)

spent the day uploading
some heavy emotions to the cloud,
so i might stop carrying this IRL weight
here on earth

my phone screen cracked last winter
yet here i am, still, in the
scorching daylight of summer
being sad on the internet

some people might call me a hero,
but i simply feel duty bound
to keeping up appearances
for my virtual constituents

after all, it is common knowledge
that the best way to process
complex emotions is to create
extremely relatable memes
born from the abyss of your
deepest, most traumatic
neuroses

you could buzz feed a whole community
with the content farm you have cultivated

growing mighty, soaring clickbait in the crop fields
to be harvested by millennial skeletons
in baggy jeans and ripped KoЯn t-shirts

in the future, digital gravestones
will patiently sit in winzip folders
held in the archaic underground annals of
online cemeteries

iMessage my condolences:
black heart emoji, wilting flower emoji,
single teardrop emoji etc.

something
that resembles
everything

inside your clasped hands
you keep a million small black bats
with furious echolalic gnawing

tell me the words you'd prefer,
like inscriptions in a burned down church
or a lonely planet guide
to an uninhabitable asteroid

better yet
let's invent new languages out of old words,
freely broadcast its cacophony

we'd carve visceral chicken scratches hard
onto each other's ambient thighs

i rest my head in your kinetic dictionary
and we stay like this for several thousand years
until you whisper:
"you think too much when we fuck"

i commit this phrase to my internal monologue
so that i may gradually process it for the rest of my life

fresh neuroses for my garden bed,
more new words for the same old things

hole

message to all road workers:
i got something you can fill baby

riiiiiiiiight here

points to the gaping hole in my heart

dear road workers:
i love you,
for real

light

a dozen women lying on a kitchen's floor
with light spilling out of their mouths,
tenderly crack open one another
to reveal swimming pools' worth

i watch the room flood with language,
girl glossolalia overflowing
from underneath the tongues
we'd learnt to hold
in silence

new syllables press hard against
roughened skin, mapping out
the empty spaces
where violence had created
the illusion of nothingness

i hold each thread of cartographical evidence
close to me, wear it like a kevlar vest
for protection

this is how i come into the light:

not in solitude,
but in solidarity

this is why i break myself open:

so i might contribute to the brightness
in some small, flickering way

parallel

in an alternate universe
you and i are teenage girls,
fumbling through awkward silences
and difficult-to-explain hickeys

i re-narrativise our adolescence thus:
instead of trembling hands,
choked-back tears
and endless
apologies for existing

we walk slowly through the sleepy suburbs
fingers entwined in each others,
hair cut into baby-dyke bangs
rather than schoolboy crew cuts

instead of weaponising ourselves against our histories
you and i are given the privilege of nostalgia

love poem

marriage is for losers
and divorce is for sore losers

i only want
to drink cold beer
and arm wrestle you
for the rest of our entire stupid
lives

morning body

a banana smoothie
with a crushed up estrogen pill
for a healthy body and soul

the sunlight lingers on my skin
i swell and expand
fresh emergent sapling - (i can become)
something beautiful (or
maybe i already am)

but when will i burst
i wonder

o goddess
please let me
stay in the light

o goddess
please carve warmth
into my transient shape

survival body

fresh bones like a makeshift sanctuary
built on the precipice of a bottomless pit

you breathe in and out, trigger
minor earthquakes on someone's
disputed territory

the red rock falls from the red rock face,
memories clung tight to
a cliff wall slow-motion nosedive into
whatever oblivion sits below

years later, you make a home from what's left
of those disaster relics; holding tight
to the things that make you whole

world champion

when i spend days in a bathtub
i am the most capable person in this room

i am giving a well-attended TED talk
on achieving just the right water temperature

i am the metallica of eating at least one slice of toast a day,
the tony hawk of remembering to take my medication

when i spend days in a bathtub
i graciously accept award nominations
for not driving off a cliff this week

i am the foremost scholar
on not stuffing my mouth full of sleeping pills

i am this week's cover star of 'not dying' magazine

when i spend days in a bathtub
i am the world champion of not killing myself

which is enough accolade to survive

plant shop

had an epiphany in the garden centre,
a neat row of tiny plants with
white cards poking out:
thrives on neglect

realised in a previous life i was a succulent
slowly being murdered by everybody's nourishment
wondering why no one could follow
simple instructions

the garden bed inside my bone terrarium
is filled with dying plants piled on top of one another
scrambling for a private, quiet
burial

each one killed so carelessly by people
who think "affection" and "care"
are interchangeable words

sitting on the bus
i wondered what it might be like
to be overflowing with things that
love sunlight, love water,
love love

one day i think i will be filled
with the kind of beautiful things
that don't whisper "fuck off"
when they are touched

had an idea for a sexy text message:
let's develop a relationship dynamic
that provides adequate space for solitude
in a way that is facilitated
by supportive companionship

had an idea for a sexier text message:
i'm sorry, please delete this number

teeth

our teeth are like grappling hooks
against resistant concrete slabs,
surfaces we didn't choose
hardened by our histories

we create unmapped terrain
the cartography of our cocks and
our cunts defying the lines they've
drawn around our bodies
to keep us from ever touching too close

every ungodly orgasm
like a cum-covered middle finger
to those who'd rather we destroy ourselves
than love another

(#1)

we are sitting inside one another's ribcages, eating one another's birth certificates.

i have found that being alive is a great way to start a relationship, possibly the best way, that typically it is the being present that is more difficult.

the world feels so anxious at the moment. it feels like the only pure things left are secret gay crushes and emotional honesty.

i like you because you're always down for a high stakes game of scrabble and also for being kind to one another.
i just want to be a gentler person.

we are lying on your balcony and hear a plane flying overhead and hope the people inside it get to where they're going safely.

while attending a close friend's dead dog's funeral we see a solitary bin chicken circling vintage graves. it is looking for a dead relative. it is looking for some delicious garbage to eat. it is looking to make a new home from old things. honestly, same.

people at my university seem to hate bin chickens but it's like, what makes you so great? bin chickens used to live in the wetlands but had to migrate here because of droughts. they are survivors. everyone in my class including me rode fixies here from glebe. i don't understand this hierarchical power dynamic.

i like you because when you talk about quitting the bakery you work at you say you're gluten intolerant in a metaphysical way. bread is so important to me but i am trying to be a more empathetic person so i just giggle about it and roll my eyes a li'l bit.

i like you because you understand when i stop conversation to point out nearby dogs. bukowski said that love is a dog from hell but i think love is a dachshund pup with tiny legs that look silly when they get too excited and try to run across the park on a summer afternoon.

it feels like joy and pain are simultaneously coexisting always, in a way that is terrifying and comforting at the exact same time. searching for closure right now seems impossible, and also stupid.

i just hope we get to be in love with each other for a really long time.

doomed things

our love
is two solitary hedgehogs
finding each other in the vast woodlands
after a million years of crushing isolation

it is the brief moment of kinship they feel
before piercing each other to death with their spines
in a doomed attempt at reciprocal intimacy

it is okay to enjoy doomed things,
i remind myself whenever you kiss my forehead

first home bile

i am providing islands
for a local land baron
kept warm at night
by investment properties

the walls are not built
to withstand harsh weather
so i wrap myself in rental applications
to prepare for the winter ahead
accessorising with vestigial asbestoses

herded into all these arbitrary divisions
i watch your blood ache
for something less ephemeral
but our bodies lie ground to dust by negative gears
salaries having mostly sentimental value at this point
i wonder what will become of the monoliths

left towering over gentrified paradise;
ultra-chic burial grounds
overpopulated by millennial skeletons
crying silently into their
superannuations

promise

she is craving something like pain
wrapped in roadkill,
afraid to get her hands messy
but there's dried blood caked beneath
each fingernail

she imagines something graceful
lying dormant underneath her skin,
hopes light could exist
in the fractions between hideous organs,
somehow forgive the crime of being human

she inches on broken knees
across broken glass towards
the promise of a safe place

  outside
i. the violence of men,
ii. the trauma of the body

wonders,
does that place even exist?

can it?

memorial

i've been trying to make funeral plans,
a proper burial for the body i've
abandoned

left lying graceless in a makeshift grave
so something beautiful might take its place

how do you erase the residual things i wonder?
the jagged edge of a jawbone, my father's hands,
the way your body remembers what you refuse to

i don't want any of these things
but i won't let them dissolve either;

ungrateful host to memory,
girl in a house on a hill on fire

instead i carry this body, it is mine,
i wear its callouses like a childhood home

there is good living to be found inside one of those,
one of these

to live inside is to let the new things
press hard up against the old things,
against the emptiness, the quiet spaces,
these great isolated yet-to-be-filled's,

all that brittle-boned architecture
making room for possibility

 on the day i told my mother i was a girl,
she said it was like her son had been put in the ground

she didn't know what was
waiting to sprout in the soil

(#2)

i cried on the bus to your house again today while reading about a trans kid in the states who killed themselves, because their parents tried to send them to a religious conversion camp.

i've never wanted so badly in my entire life to be able to pour my love into another human being in a way that would somehow make it okay. i am thinking a lot about what it means to love a trans person, a trans body. it doesn't take much but it is so extremely powerful. i don't understand why it is so difficult for some people.

an old woman sitting near me on the bus saw me crying and reached out her hand and i took it and didn't say anything. she just kept holding and i just kept crying and eventually she had to get off the bus at marrickville metro and i wasn't going to hold up her grocery shopping.

i've been trying hard to be a more empathetic person. i've been trying to hold my feet on solid ground and assert myself instead of apologising for being alive. lately i feel like this earth is trying to kill me, and that my brain is trying to kill me too. but i love this earth, and i love myself, and i want to stay alive long enough for both of these things to heal. i want to believe so, so badly these things are possible.

i got off the bus and walked to your house and we read anne carson poems together in your bed. i felt held. as if i could pour my love into someone. as if that could somehow possibly be okay with the way this earth is, with the way i am. is it okay that i love you because you make me feel safe?

(i love you,
because you make me feel safe.)

AUTHOR ACKNOWLEDGEMENTS

Thank you to Rory Green, Nina Dodd, Katherine
Giunta, Joseph Thomas, Erin Violet, Jonno Revanche,
Zoe Lane, Dan Hogan & Stacey Teague.

ABOUT THE AUTHOR

Alex Gallagher is a Sydney-based writer and poet.
Their poems have appeared in places like Overland,
Scum and Potluck Mag, while essays and other writing
have appeared in the *Sydney Morning Herald*, *Kill Your
Darlings*, *Southerly* and *Junkee*.

'vague', 'morning body' and 'survival body' first
published by *Potluck Magazine*. 'teeth' first published
in *Concrete Queers* #6. 'something that resembles
everything' first published by *Scum Mag*. 'parallel' first
published by *Moonsick Magazine*. 'first home bile' first
published in *Overland* #227. Dedication appears in
Hannahband's 'G Morals' (*Retirement*, 2015).

Subbed In is a not-for-profit DIY literary organisation and small press based in Sydney, Australia. Subbed In's program of publications and events aim to elevate the voices of trans people, people of colour, non-binary people, sex workers, women, people with a disability, LGBTQIA+ people, First Nations people, survivors, working class people, and anyone who finds themselves on the margins of the supremely white, cis, heteronormative, capitalist, colonial, ableist, patriarchal hellscape in which we live.

For more information visit: *www.subbed.in*

ALSO AVAILABLE FROM SUBBED IN

Printed in Australia
AUHW010939291019
319226AU00002B/7